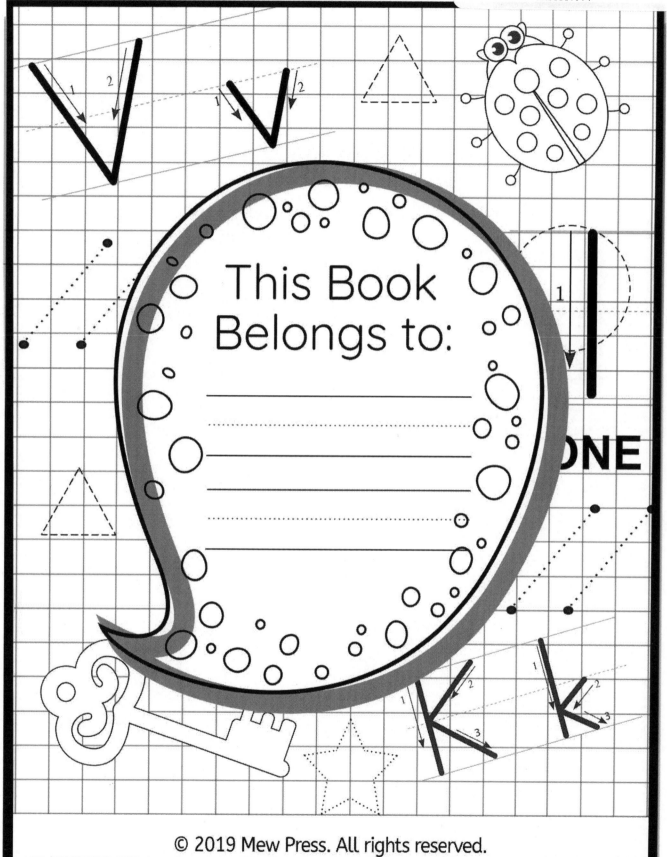

This Book Belongs to:

_____

_____

_____

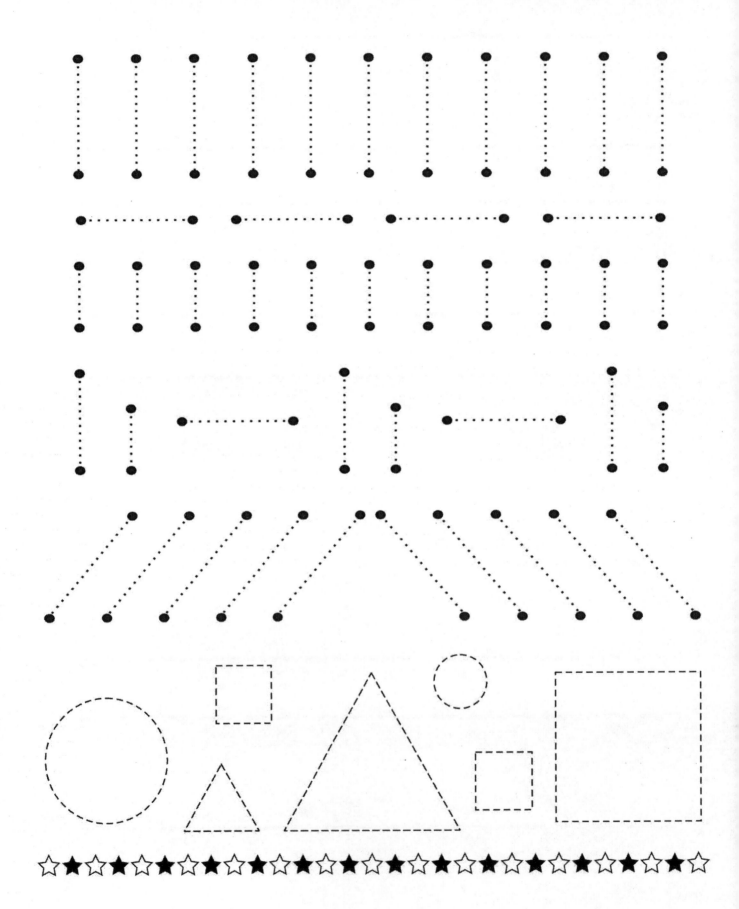

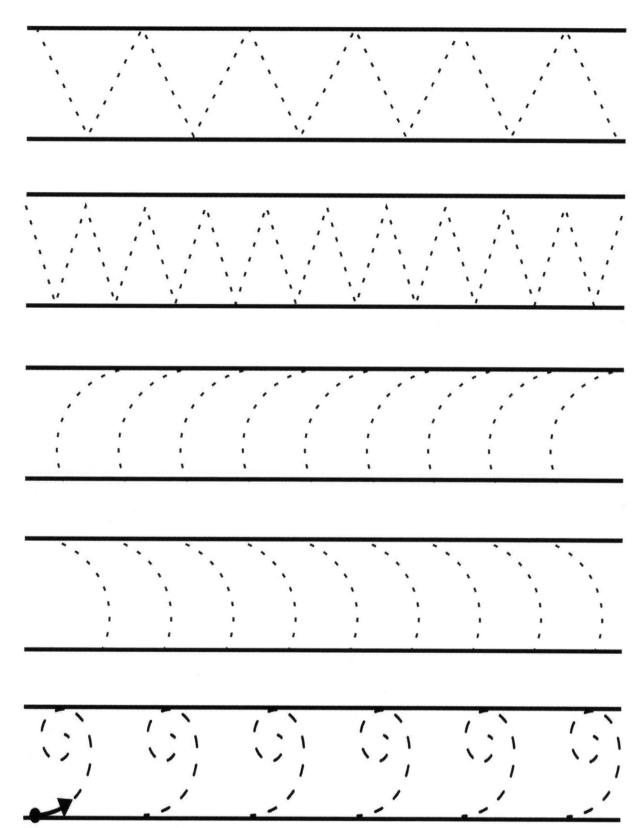

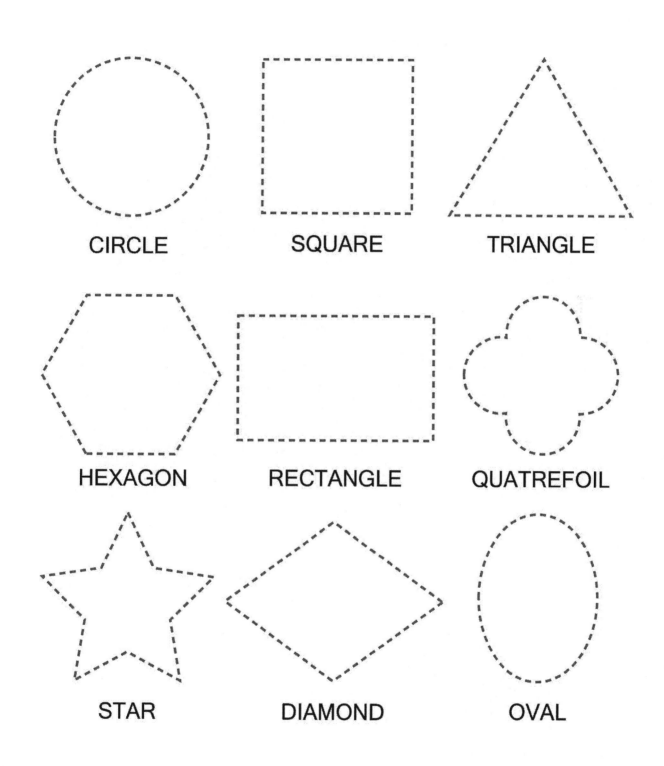

CIRCLE · SQUARE · TRIANGLE

HEXAGON · RECTANGLE · QUATREFOIL

STAR · DIAMOND · OVAL

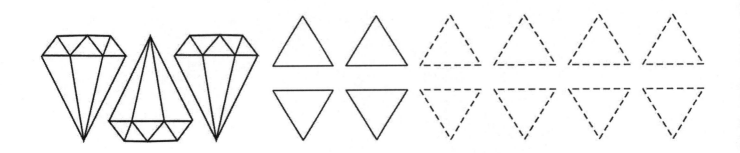

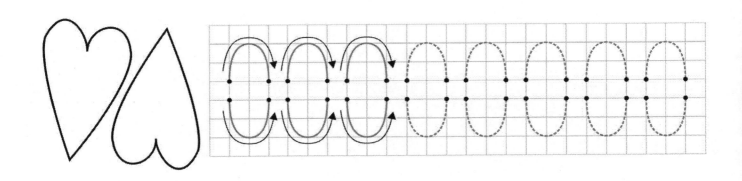

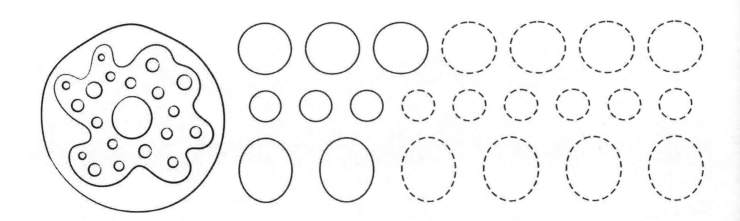

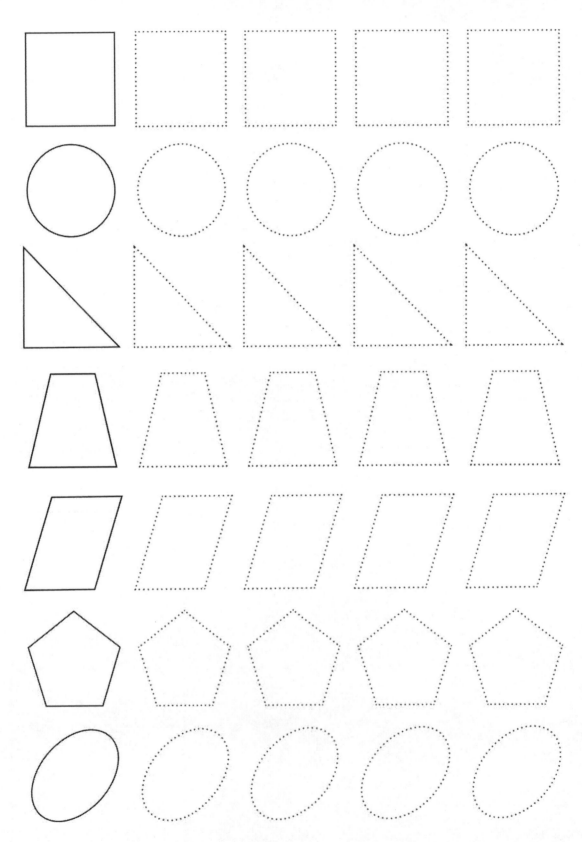

A is for AIRPLANE

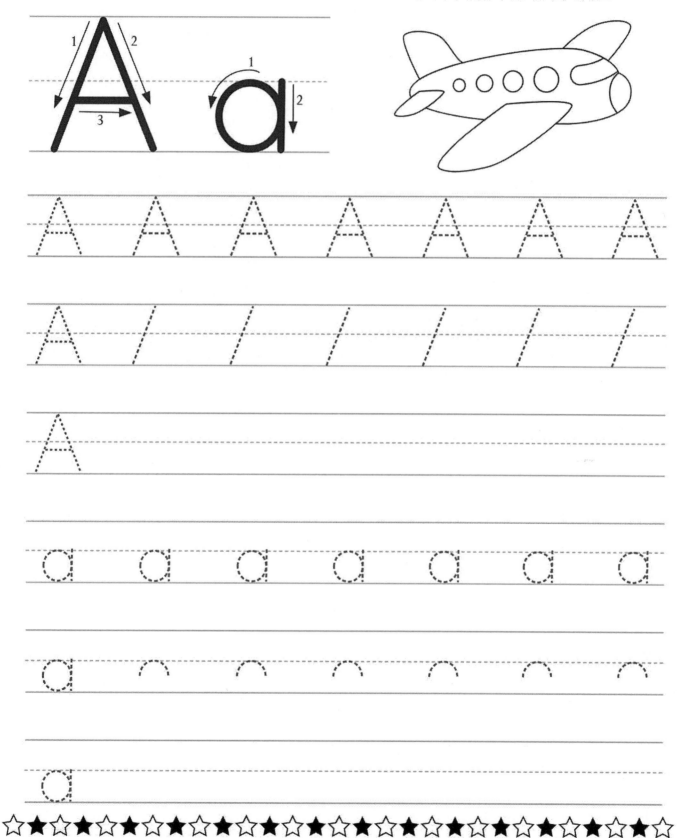

☆★☆★☆★☆★☆★☆★☆★☆★☆★☆★☆★☆★☆★☆★☆

☆★☆★☆★☆★☆★☆★☆★☆★☆★☆★☆★☆★☆★☆★☆

A is for Aquarium

B b

B is for BUTTERFLY

B B B B B B B B

B ⌐ ⌐ ⌐ ⌐ ⌐ ⌐ ⌐

B

b b b b b b b

b r r r r r r r

b

☆★☆★☆★☆★☆★☆★☆★☆★☆★☆★☆★☆★☆★☆

B is for Bunny

C is for CROWN

☆★☆★☆★☆★☆★☆★☆★☆★☆★☆★☆★☆★☆★☆

☆★☆★☆★☆★☆★☆★☆★☆★☆★☆★☆★☆★☆★☆

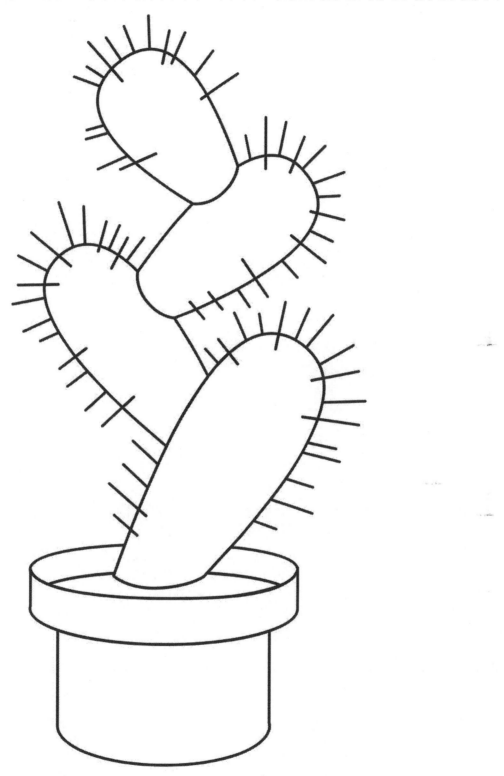

C is for Cactus

D is for DUCK

D d

D is for Doll

E is for ENVELOPE

E is for Easter

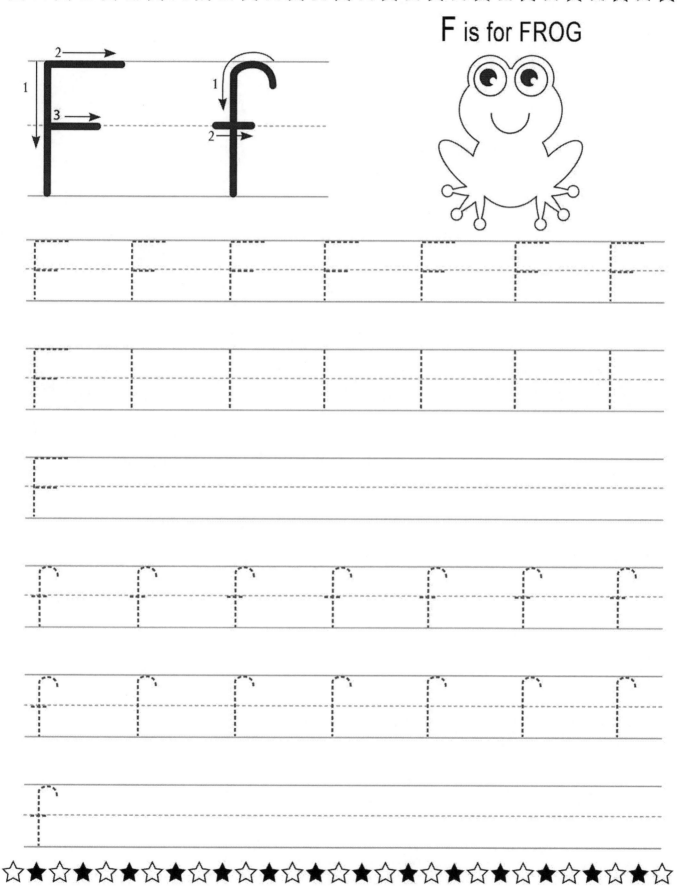

F is for FROG

F is for Fishing

☆★☆★☆★☆★☆★☆★☆★☆★☆★☆★☆★☆★☆★☆★☆★☆

G is for GOAT

G g

G G G G G G G G

G G G G G G G G

G

g g g g g g g

g g g g g g g

g

☆★☆★☆★☆★☆★☆★☆★☆★☆★☆★☆★☆★☆★☆★☆★☆

G is for Giraffe

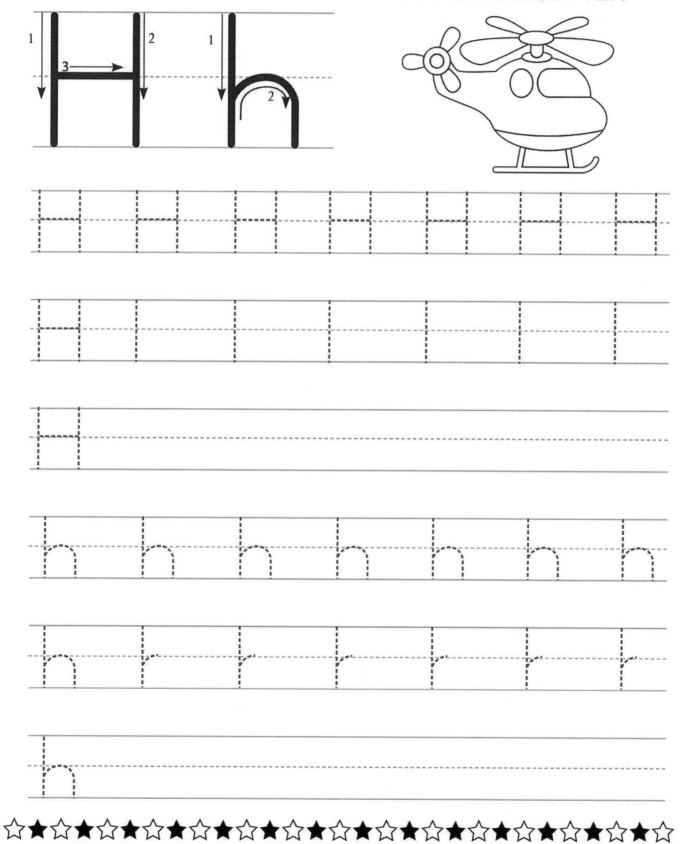

H is for HELICOPTER

H is for Hamburger

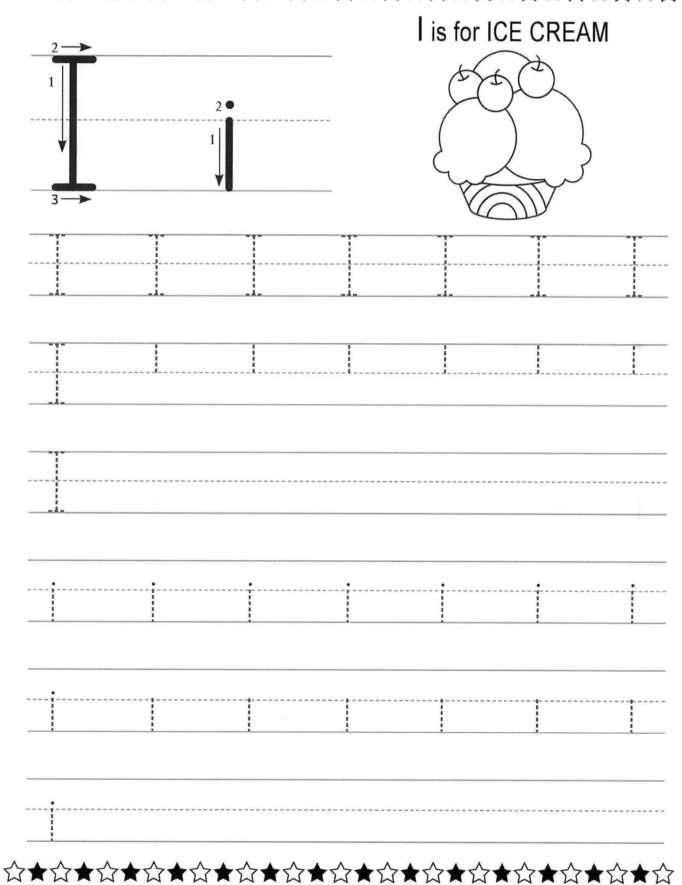

I is for ICE CREAM

☆★☆★☆★☆★☆★☆★☆★☆★☆★☆★☆★☆★☆★☆★☆

I is for Iguana

J is for JAM

J is for Jellyfish

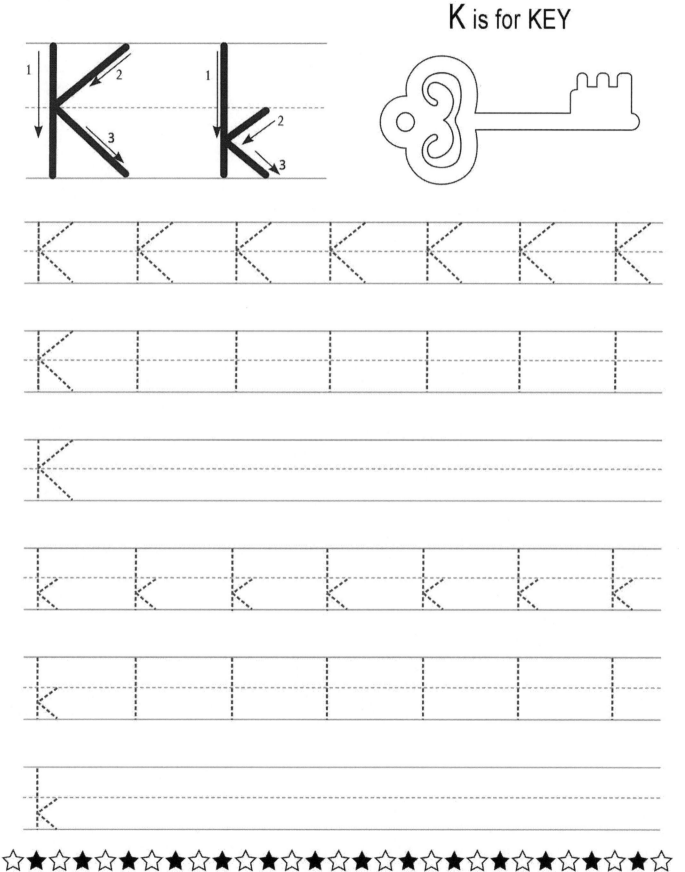

K is for KEY

K is for Koala

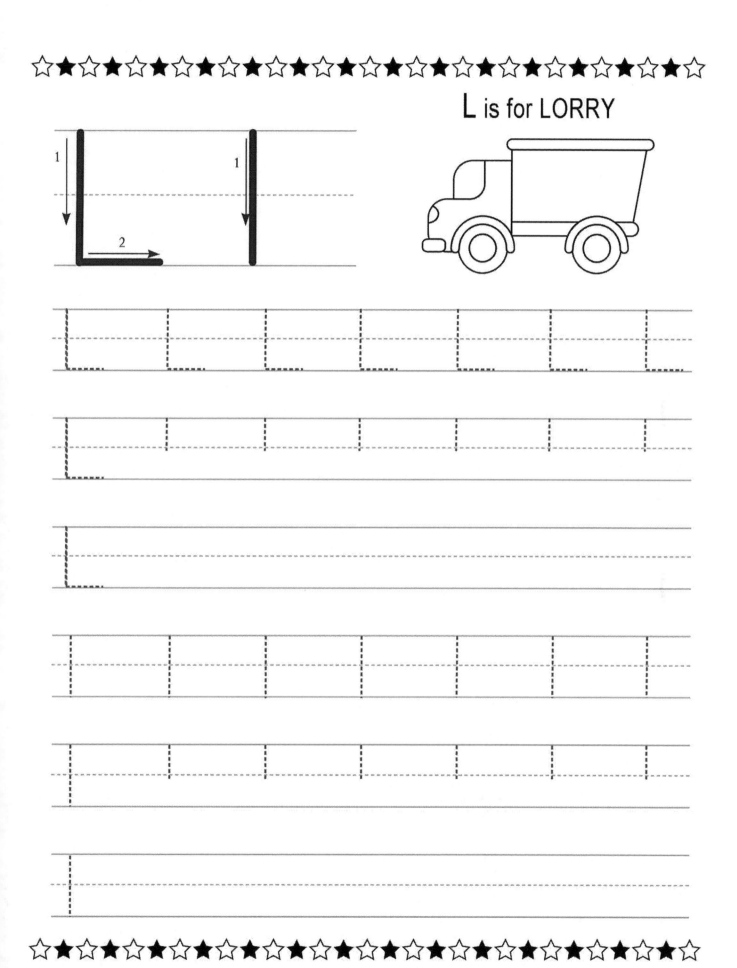

L is for LORRY

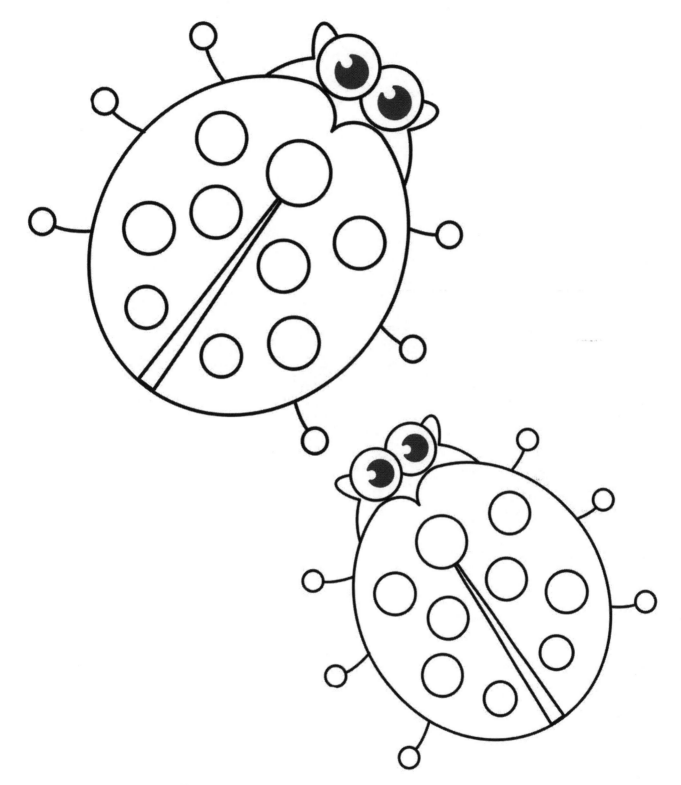

L is for Ladybug

M is for MUSHROOM

M is for Monkey

N is for NOTE

N is for Necklace

O is for ORANGE

O is for Owl

P is for PANDA

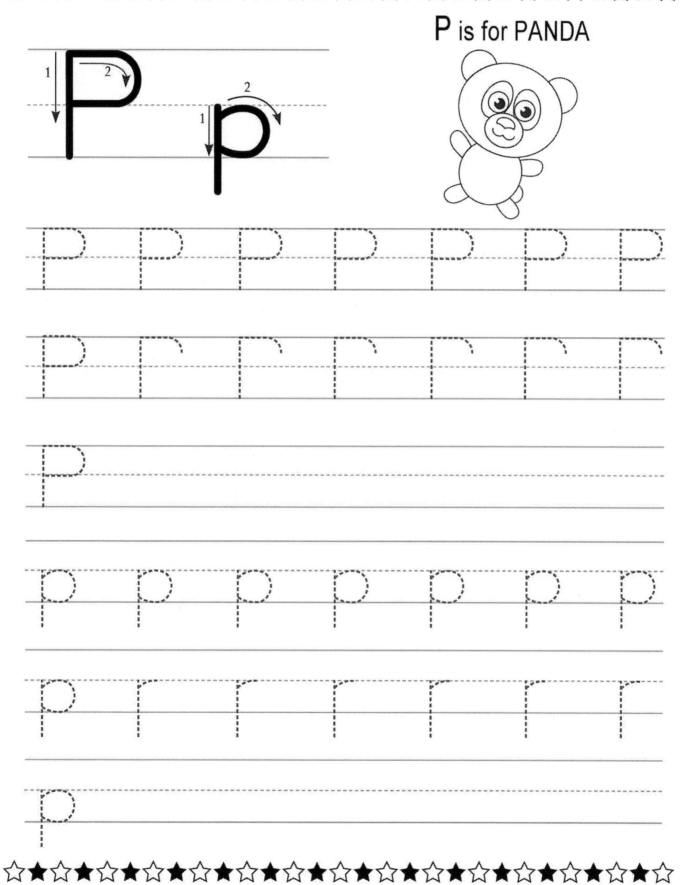

P is for Pizza

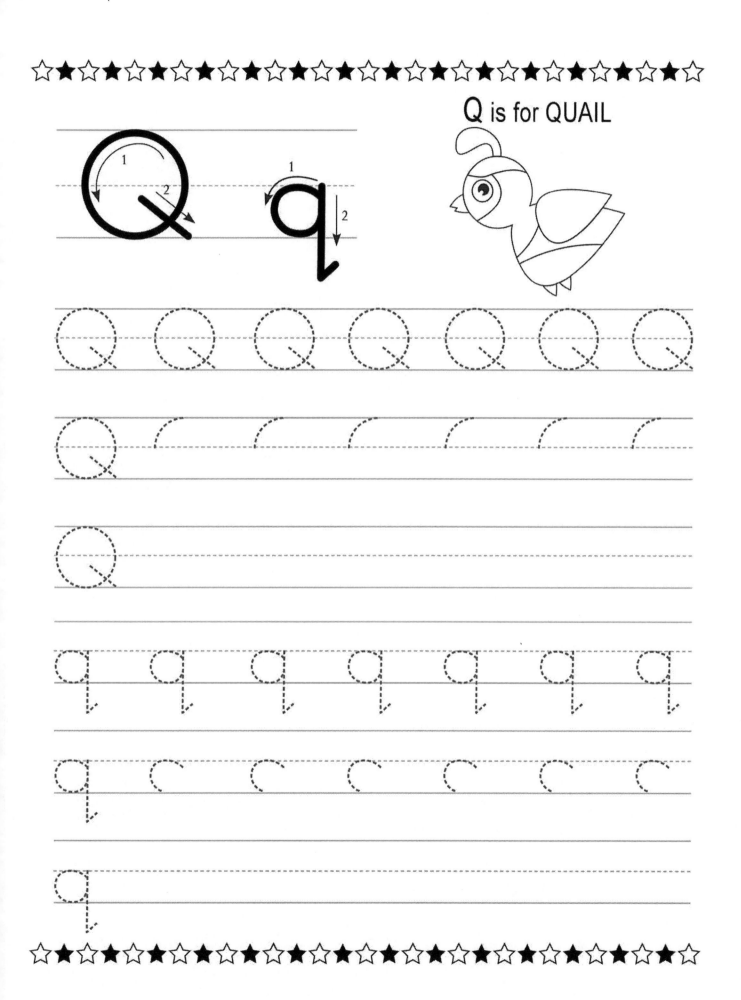

Q is for QUAIL

☆★☆★☆★☆★☆★☆★☆★☆★☆★☆★☆★☆★☆★☆★☆

☆★☆★☆★☆★☆★☆★☆★☆★☆★☆★☆★☆★☆★☆★☆

Q is for Queen Bee

R is for RAINBOW

☆★☆★☆★☆★☆★☆★☆★☆★☆★☆★☆★☆★☆

☆★☆★☆★☆★☆★☆★☆★☆★☆★☆★☆★☆★☆

R is for Rocket

S is for STEGOSAURUS

S is for Snail

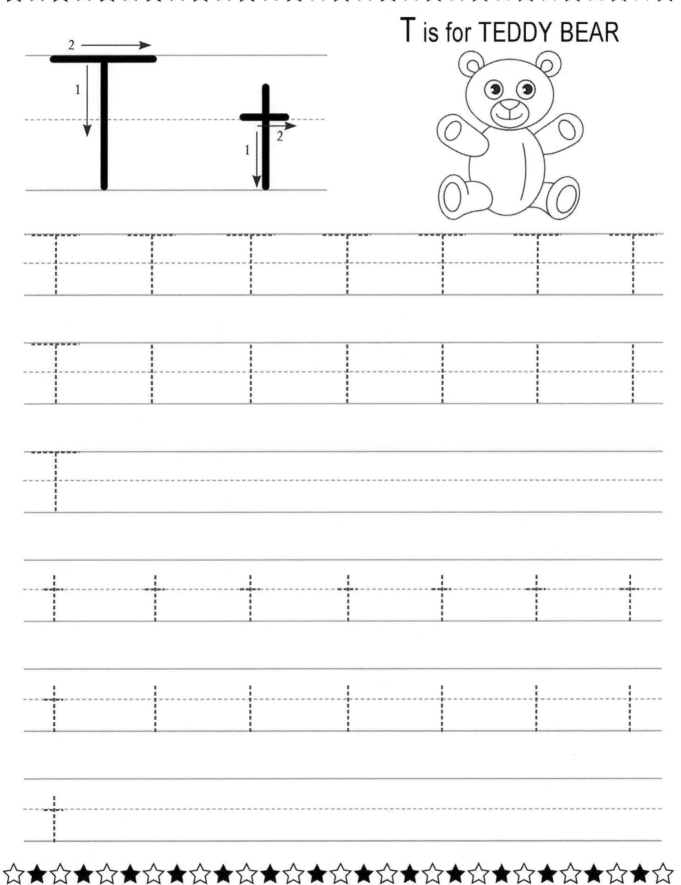

T is for TEDDY BEAR

☆★☆★☆★☆★☆★☆★☆★☆★☆★☆★☆★☆★☆

★☆★☆★☆★☆★☆★☆★☆★☆★☆★☆★☆★☆★☆

T is for Tiger

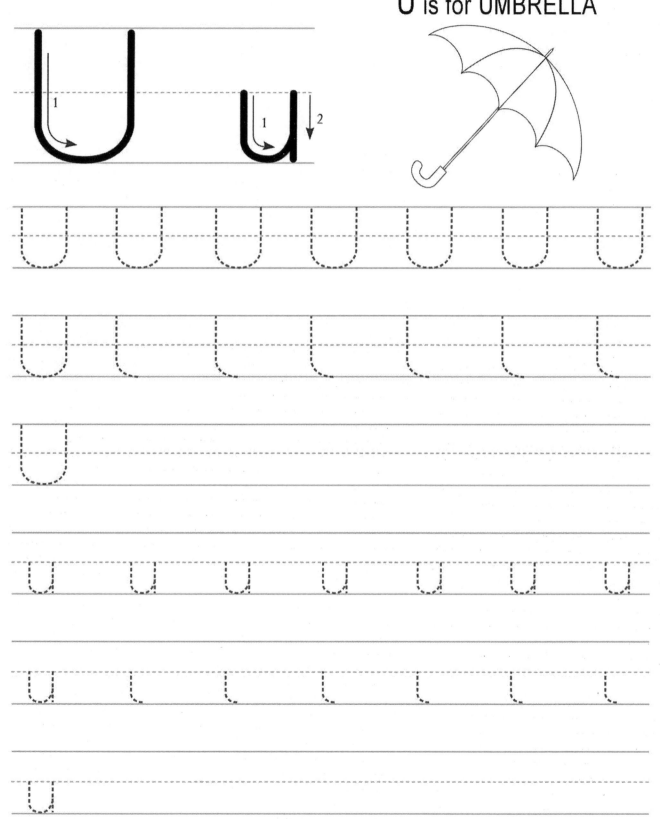

U is for UMBRELLA

U is for Unicorn

☆★☆★☆★☆★☆★☆★☆★☆★☆★☆★☆★☆★☆★☆★☆★☆★☆

V is for VASE

V ✏️¹ ² V ¹ ²

V V V V V V V

V V V V V V V

V

V V V V V V V

V V V V V V

V

☆★☆★☆★☆★☆★☆★☆★☆★☆★☆★☆★☆★☆★☆★☆★☆★☆

☆★☆★☆★☆★☆★☆★☆★☆★☆★☆★☆★☆★☆★☆★☆

☆★☆★☆★☆★☆★☆★☆★☆★☆★☆★☆★☆★☆★☆★☆

V is for Vampire Bat

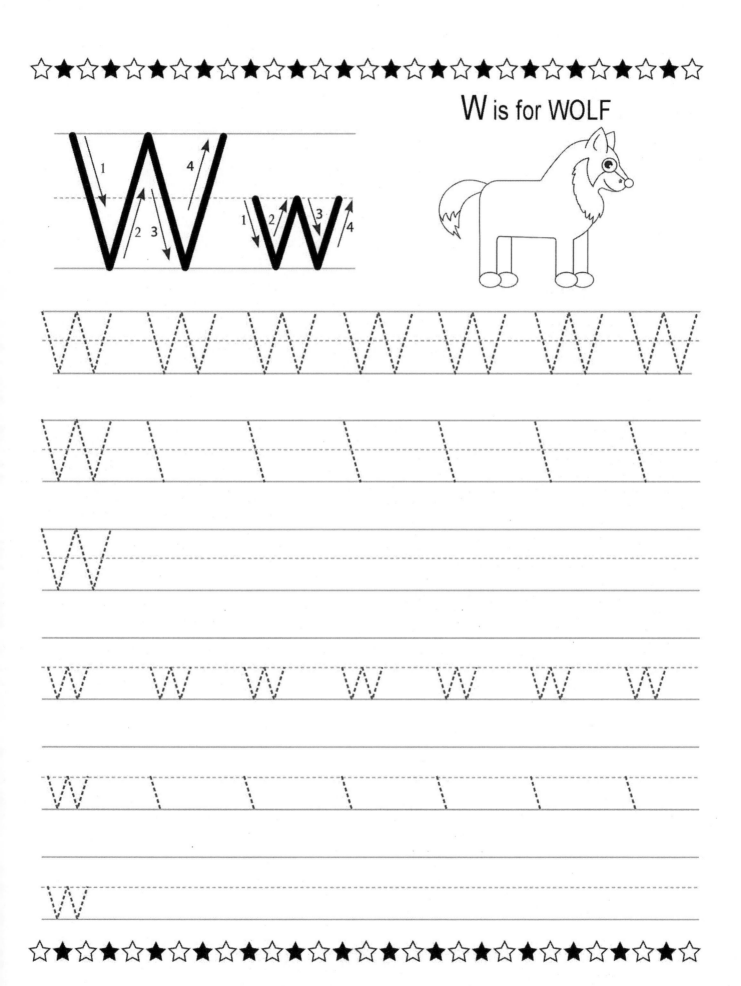

W is for WOLF

☆★☆★☆★☆★☆★☆★☆★☆★☆★☆★☆★☆★☆★☆★☆
☆★☆★☆★☆★☆★☆★☆★☆★☆★☆★☆★☆★☆★☆★☆

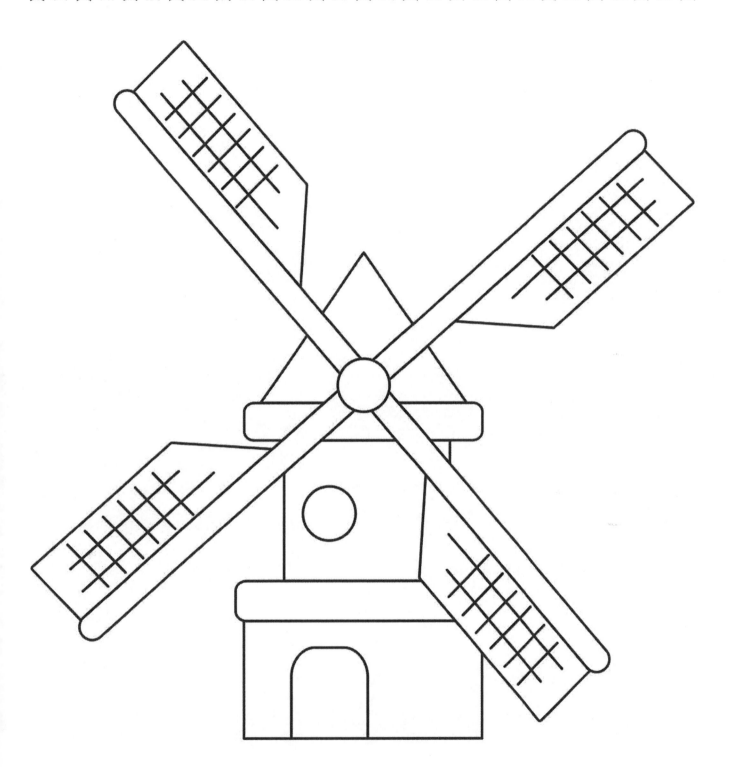

W is for Windmill

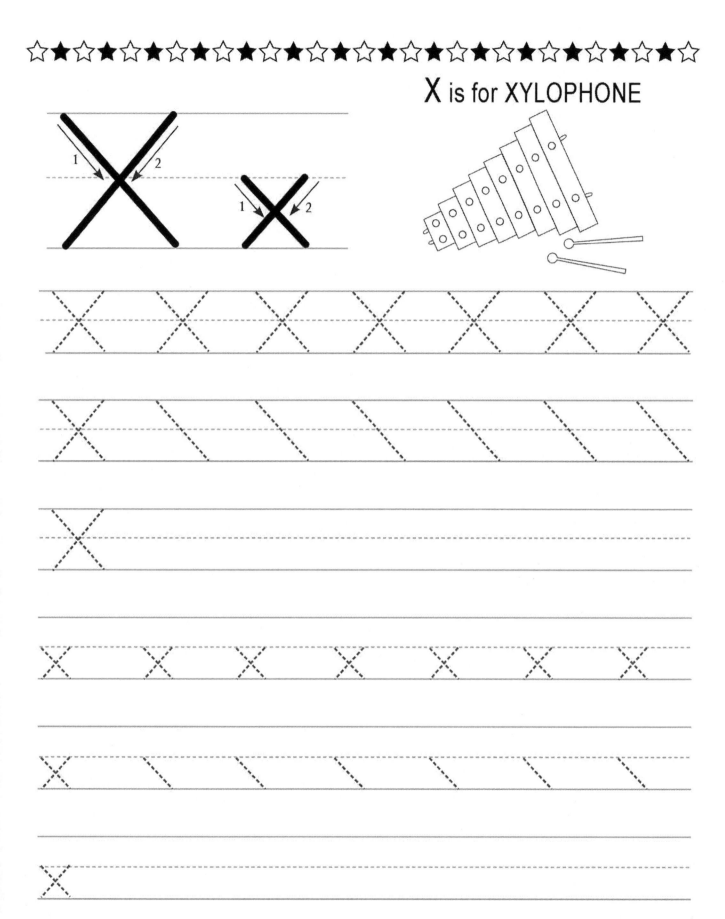

X is for XYLOPHONE

X is for Xmas

Y is for YARN

Y is for Yak

Z is for ZIPPER

Z is for Zebra

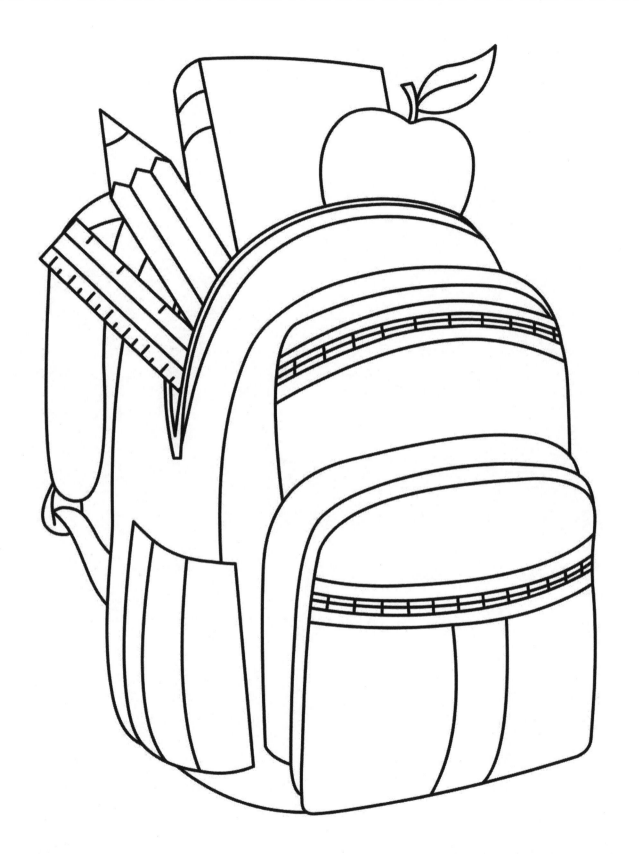

What comes next?

A B C B A B [?]

J K L L K J [?]

S T T U T T [?]

X Y Z X Y Z [?]

Aa Bb Cc Dd Ee

Ff Gg Hh Ii Jj

Kk Ll Mm Nn

Oo Pp Qq Rr

Ss Tt Uu Vv

Ww Xx Yy Zz

ONE

2

TWO

☆★☆★☆★☆★☆★☆★☆★☆★☆★☆★☆★☆★☆★☆★☆★☆★☆

3

1
2

THREE

3 3 3 3 3 3 3

3 2 2 2 2 2 2

3

3

3

☆★☆★☆★☆★☆★☆★☆★☆★☆★☆★☆★☆★☆★☆★☆★☆★☆

4

1
2
3

FOUR

5

FIVE

6
SIX

☆★☆★☆★☆★☆★☆★☆★☆★☆★☆★☆★☆★☆★☆★☆★☆★

☆★☆★☆★☆★☆★☆★☆★☆★☆★☆★☆★☆★☆★☆★☆★☆★

7

SEVEN

8

1 → ← 4
3 → ← 2

EIGHT

8 8 8 8 8 8 8

8 5 5 5 5 5 5

8

8

8

☆★☆★☆★☆★☆★☆★☆★☆★☆★☆★☆★☆★☆★☆

☆★☆★☆★☆★☆★☆★☆★☆★☆★☆★☆★☆★☆★☆

q

NINE

q q q q q q q

q c c c c c c

q

q

q

☆★☆★☆★☆★☆★☆★☆★☆★☆★☆★☆★☆★☆★☆★

☆★☆★☆★☆★☆★☆★☆★☆★☆★☆★☆★☆★☆★☆★

10

TEN

1. $2 + 1 + \boxed{} = 6$

2. $5 + \boxed{} - 1 = 8$

3. $9 - 4 + 2 = \boxed{}$

4. $\boxed{} - 3 - 1 = 5$

5. $7 + 4 - \boxed{} = 9$

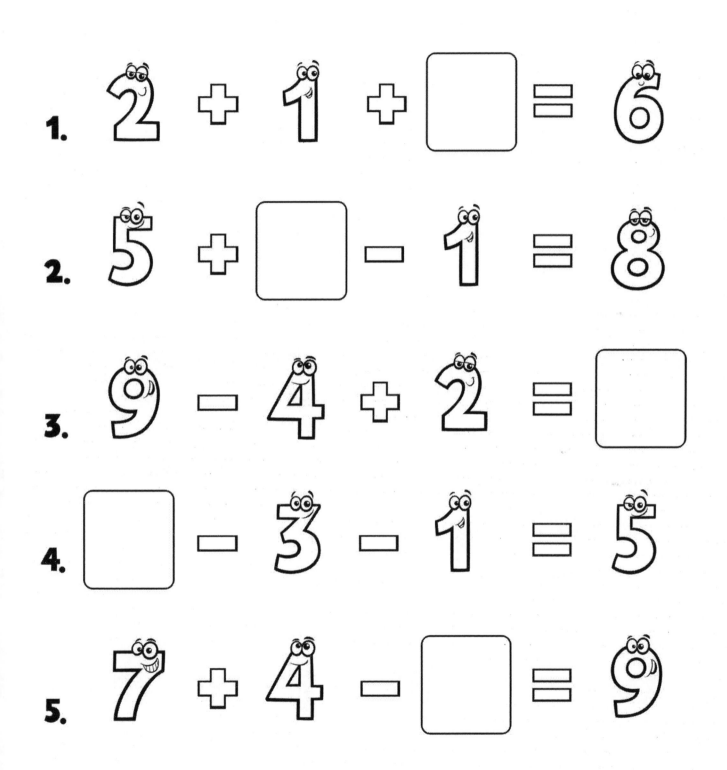

Draw the hands on the clock to show the time

1:30   5:00   3:15

12:30   6:45   7:30

11:00   8:15   2:30

1 = yellow   4 = green   7 = orange
2 = red   5 = blue   8 = brown
3 = pink   6 = purple

Color **first** , **third**, **sixth** and **seventh** flowers

Color **second** , **third**, **fifth** and **ninth** stars

Color **second** , **fourth**, **sixth** , **eighth** and **tenth** hearts

Color **first** , **third**, **sixth** and **seventh** hearts

Color the circle with the correct answer

⭐⭐⭐⭐⭐ + ⭐⭐⭐⭐⭐ = (8) (10) (5)

●●●● + ●●● = (7) (9) (6)

♥♥♥♥ + ♥♥♥♥♥ = (8) (10) (9)

■■■ + ■■ = (6) (4) (5)

▲▲▲▲▲ + ▲▲ = (5) (7) (9)

✿✿✿✿ + ✿✿✿✿ = (8) (10) (5)

❀❀❀ + ❀❀❀ = (3) (6) (4)

How many?

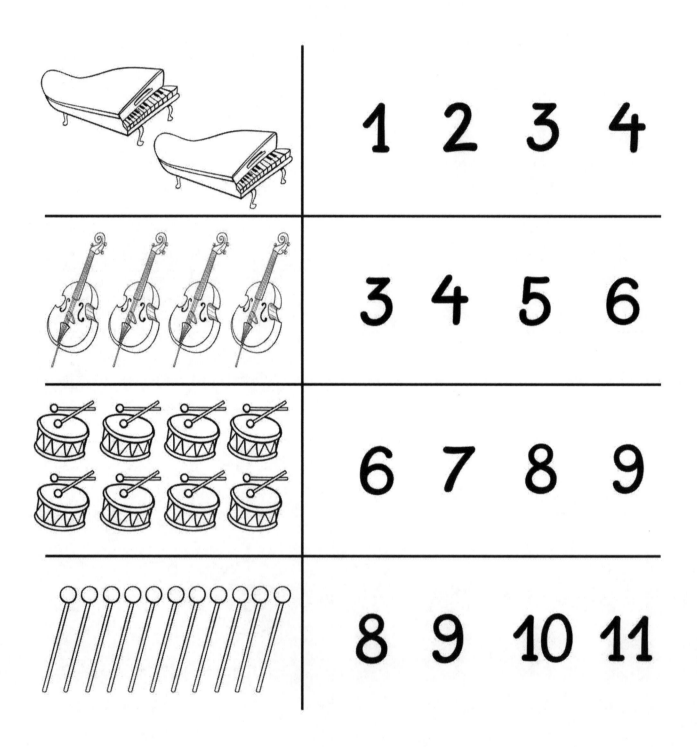

☆★☆★☆★☆★☆★☆★☆★☆★☆★☆★☆★☆★☆★☆★☆

☆★☆★☆★☆★☆★☆★☆★☆★☆★☆★☆★☆★☆

☆★☆★☆★☆★☆★☆★☆★☆★☆★☆★☆★☆★☆

☆★☆★☆★☆★☆★☆★☆★☆★☆★☆★☆★☆★☆★☆★

☆★☆★☆★☆★☆★☆★☆★☆★☆★☆★☆★☆★☆★☆★

☆★☆★☆★☆★☆★☆★☆★☆★☆★☆★☆★☆★☆★☆★☆★☆

★☆★☆★☆★☆★☆★☆★☆★☆★☆★☆★☆★☆★☆★☆★☆★☆

☆★☆★☆★☆★☆★☆★☆★☆★☆★☆★☆★☆★☆★☆★☆

TRACING
For Toddlers

Age 2+

Beginner to Tracing Lines
Shapes & ABC Letters

Fun Kids Tracing Book

Made in the USA
Columbia, SC
08 April 2020